W9-CNZ-057

WONDERFULLY

Whimsical Quilts

10 Playful Projects to Make You Smile

CAROL BURNISTON

C&T PUBLISHING

Text © 2005 Carol Burniston

Artwork © 2005 C&T Publishing

Publisher: Amy Marson

Editorial Director: Gailen Runge

Aquisitions Editor: Jan Grigsby

Editor: Darra Williamson

Technical Editors: Teresa Stroin, Gael Betts, and Gayl Gallagher

Copyeditor: Stacy Chamness

Proofreader: Wordfirm

Cover Designer: Christina D. Jarumay

Design Director/Book Designer: Christina D. Jarumay

Illustrator: John Heisch

Production Assistant: Kirstie L. McCormick

Photography: Sharon Risedorph

Published by C&T Publishing, Inc., P.O. Box 1456, Lafayette, CA, 94549

Front cover: *Happy Cats*

Back cover: *Party Fish, Outside the Box, Hot Tamale Sunflowers, Sheep in Dreamland, Quack Quack,* and *Flowers on the Vine,* by Carol Burniston

All rights reserved. No part of this work covered by the copyright hereon may be reproduced or used in any form or any means—graphic, electronic, or mechanical, including photocopying, recording, taping, or information storage and retrieval systems—without written permission of the publisher. The copyrights on individual artworks are retained by the artists as noted in *Wonderfully Whimsical Quilts.*

Attention Copy Shops: Please note the following exception—Publisher and author give permission to photocopy pages 8, 9, 13, 17, 18, 22, 28, 29, 32, 33, 37, 40, 43 for personal use only.

Attention Teachers: C&T Publishing, Inc. encourages you to use this book as a text for teaching. Contact us at 800-284-1114 or www.ctpub.com for more information about the C&T Teachers Program.

We take great care to ensure that the information included in this book is accurate and presented in good faith, but no warranty is provided nor results guaranteed. Having no control over the choices of materials or procedures used, neither the author nor C&T Publishing, Inc. shall have any liability to any person or entity with respect to any loss or damage caused directly or indirectly by the information contained in this book. For your convenience, we post an up-to-date listing of corrections on our web page (www.ctpub.com). If a correction is not already noted, please contact our customer service department at ctinfo@ctpub.com or at P.O. Box 1456, Lafayette, CA, 94549.

Trademarked (™) and Registered Trademark (®) names are used throughout this book. Rather than use the symbols with every occurrence of a trademark and registered trademark name, we are using the names only in the editorial fashion and to the benefit of the owner, with no intention of infringement.

Library of Congress Cataloging-in-Publication Data

Burniston, Carol.

Wonderfully whimsical quilts : 10 playful projects to make you smile / Carol Burniston.

   p. cm.

  ISBN 1-57120-271-4 (paper trade)

  1. Appliqué--Patterns. 2. Patchwork--Patterns. 3. Quilting. I. Title.

TT779.B7746 2004

  746.46'041--dc22

                        2004014471

Printed in China

10 9 8 7 6 5 4 3 2 1

DEDICATION

To my mother, Bessie Anderson.

ACKNOWLEDGMENTS

Thank you to my family for your support and encouragement.

Brittany, welcome to our family!

CONTENTS

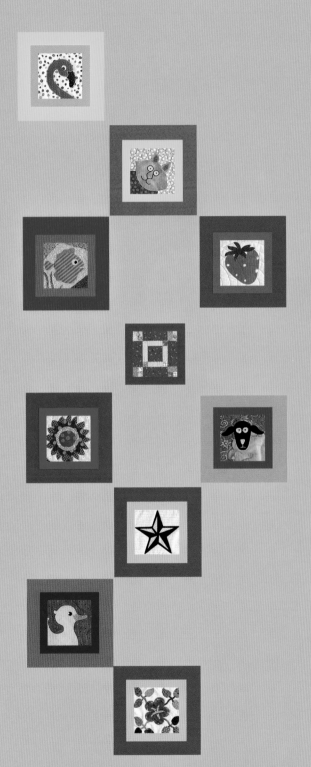

I 've designed and created this collection of quilts to be lighthearted and playful; there's nothing stuffy here—just wonderful fabrics and a touch of whimsy in the design. For me, quilting has always been more about fun than perfection.

I love color, especially in unexpected combinations. (I just redecorated my family room in hot pink, lime green, and aqua.) It's the colorful, silly prints that catch my eye. One of the hottest trends in fabric right now is the bright, cheerful novelty print, and my patterns show you how to use these fun fabrics. Quilt stores offer so many fabulous choices; you won't have any trouble finding great fabrics of your own to work with.

Don't be intimidated by the non-traditional construction of these quilts. Thanks to fusible appliqué and easy piecing, you'll find them surprisingly simple to make. I hope you have as much fun making them as I did!

Carol

Flamingos in Paradise

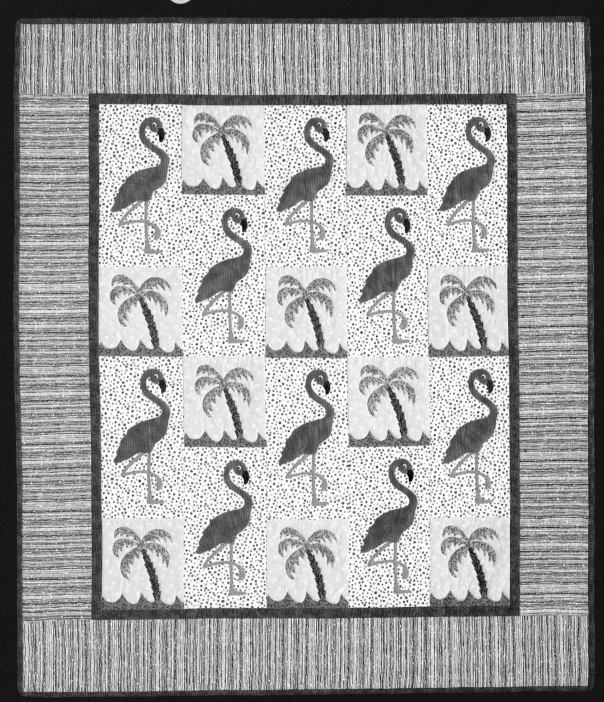

FLAMINGOS IN PARADISE

DESIGNED AND MADE BY CAROL BURNISTON,
MACHINE QUILTED BY JANET MURDOCK.
FINISHED QUILT: **56″** × **64″**
FINISHED BLOCKS: **8″** × **15½″** AND **8″** × **8½″**

Materials You'll Need

1⅔ yards white dotted print for Flamingo block background

1¼ yards yellow print for Palm Tree block background

1⅛ yards purple subtle print or solid for inner border and binding

1¾ yards multicolored stripe for outer border

1 yard pink print for flamingo appliqués

¾ yard orange pin dot for flamingo appliqués

⅛ yard navy blue print for flamingo appliqués

Scraps of white solid for flamingo appliqués

½ yard green print for palm tree appliqués

¼ yard brown print for palm tree appliqués

¼ yard aqua blue print for palm tree appliqués

3⅞ yards fabric for backing

64″ × 72″ piece of batting

6 yards lightweight 22″-wide fusible web

Thread to match appliqués

Cutting the Fabric

Cut strips from the crosswise grain of the fabric.

From the white dotted print, cut:

5 strips, 8½″ × 40″; crosscut into 10 blocks, 8½″ × 16″

From the yellow print, cut:

3 strips, 8½″ × 40″; crosscut into 10 blocks, 8½″ × 9″

From the purple print, cut:

5 strips, 1½″ × 40″

7 strips, 3″ × 40″

From the multicolored stripe, cut:

6 strips, 7½″ × 40″

Appliquéing the Flamingo and Palm Tree Blocks

You need 20 appliquéd blocks: 10 Flamingo blocks and 10 Palm Tree blocks. Refer to Fusible Appliqué on page 45.

1. Use the patterns on pages 8–9 to trace and cut 10 A from the pink print; 10 each of B and C from the orange pin dot; 10 each of D and E from the navy blue print; 10 F from the white solid; 10 G from the green print; 10 H from the brown print; and 10 I from the aqua blue print.

> *Depending upon the fabric, you may be able to cut the eye of the flamingo (E–F) as a single piece (E) from one of the dots in the white dotted fabric.*

2. Refer to the flamingo appliqué placement diagram below. Position 1 each of A–F on each 8½″ × 16″ white dotted block. Fuse in place. Make 10 blocks.

3. Refer to the palm tree appliqué placement diagram. Position 1 each of G–I on each 8½″ × 9″ yellow block. Fuse in place. Make 10 blocks.

4. Finish the edges of the appliqués with matching-colored thread and a machine blanket stitch.

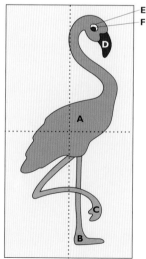 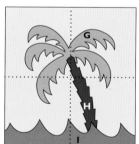

Appliqué placement diagrams
Make 10 of each block.

Assembling the Quilt

1. Refer to the quilt assembly diagram. Lay out the Flamingo and Palm Tree blocks in five vertical rows, alternating the blocks as shown.

2. Sew the blocks into rows. Press.

3. Sew the rows together. Press the seams in one direction. The quilt should measure 40½" × 48½".

4. Refer to Adding Borders on page 46. Sew the 1½"-wide purple strips end-to-end to make one continuous border strip. From this strip, cut 2 strips 1½" × 48½" for the side borders and 2 strips 1½" × 42½" for the top and bottom borders.

5. Sew the 1½" × 48½" strips to the sides of the quilt. Press the seams toward the border strips. Sew the 1½" × 42½" strips to the top and bottom of the quilt. Press.

6. Repeat Steps 4 and 5 to piece, measure, cut, and sew the 7½"-wide multicolored striped borders to the quilt. Press the seams toward the purple borders.

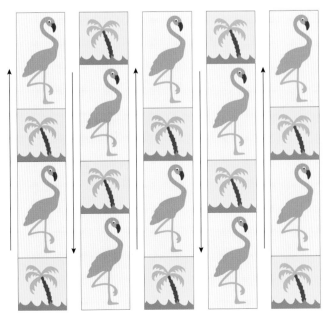

Quilt assembly diagram

Quilting and Binding

Refer to Basic Quiltmaking Instructions (pages 44–48) as needed to finish your quilt.

1. Divide the backing fabric in half selvage to selvage, reseam, and trim to make a 64" × 72" backing. Layer the quilt top, batting, and backing. Baste the three layers.

2. Quilt as desired.

3. Make binding using the 3"-wide purple strips and finish the edges of the quilt.

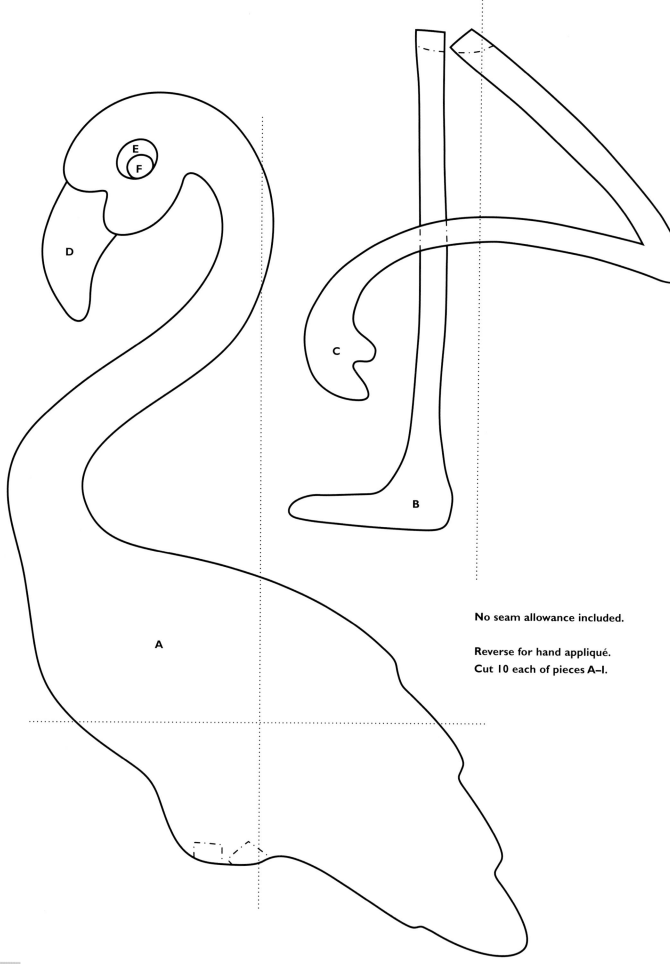

D

E
F

C

B

A

No seam allowance included.

Reverse for hand appliqué.
Cut 10 each of pieces A–I.

Happy Cats

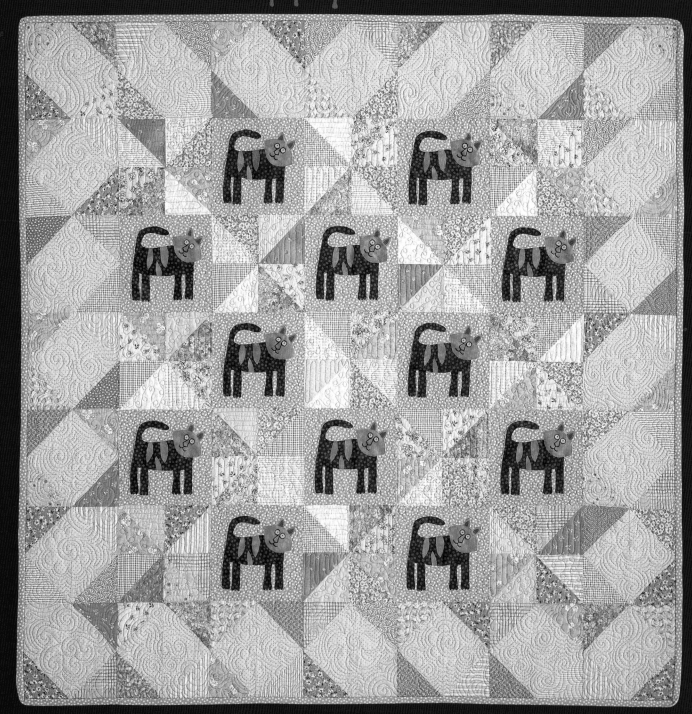

HAPPY CATS

DESIGNED AND MADE BY CAROL BURNISTON,

MACHINE QUILTED BY JANET MURDOCK.

FINISHED QUILT: **63″ × 63″**

FINISHED BLOCK: **9″ SQUARE**

Materials You'll Need

2¼ yards pink print #1 for appliqué background and
  binding

3 yards total assorted pink prints for Pinwheel and
  border blocks

1½ yards yellow print for border blocks

1 yard blue print for cat appliqués

⅝ yard lime green print for cat appliqués

Scraps of yellow and red prints for cat appliqués

4¼ yards fabric for backing

71″ × 71″ piece of batting

3¾ yards lightweight 22″-wide fusible web

Thread to match appliqués

Black embroidery floss

 # Cutting the Fabric

Cut strips from the crosswise grain of the fabric.

From pink print #1, cut:

3 strips, 9½″ × 40″; crosscut into 12 squares, 9½″ × 9½″

7 strips, 3″ × 40″

From the assorted pink prints, cut:

100 squares, 5⅜″ × 5⅜″

From the yellow print, cut:

7 strips, 5⅜″ × 40″; crosscut into 48 squares, 5⅜″ × 5⅜″

 # Appliquéing the Cat Blocks

You need 12 appliquéd blocks. Refer to Fusible
Appliqué on page 45.

1. Use the patterns on page 13 to trace and cut 12 A
from the blue print, 12 each of B–E from the green print,
24 F from the yellow scraps, and 12 each of G and H
from the red scraps.

2. Use pattern B to trace the cat's face on each B piece.
Refer to the photo on page 10 as needed.

3. Refer to the appliqué placement diagram below.
Position 1 each of A–E, G, and H; and 2 of F on each
9½″ pink square. Fuse in place. Make 12 blocks.

4. Finish the edges of the appliqués with matching-
colored thread and a machine blanket stitch.

5. Refer to Embroidery Stitches on page 46. Use two
strands of black embroidery floss and a backstitch to
embroider each cat's nose and mouth, and around each
eye. Make a French knot in the center of each eye.

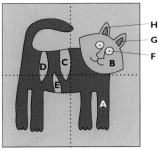

Appliqué placement diagram
Make 12 blocks.

 # Piecing the Pinwheel Blocks

1. Mark a diagonal line on the wrong side of 26 of the
5⅜″ pink squares. Place a marked square, right sides
together, with an unmarked 5⅜″ pink square.

Make 26.

2. Sew ¼″ on each side of the drawn line. Cut on the
drawn line to make 2 half-square triangle units. Press
each unit open toward the darker fabric. Make 52 half-
square triangle units.

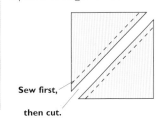

Sew first,
then cut.

Make 52.

 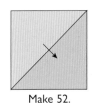

3. Arrange and sew 4 half-square triangle units as shown. Press. Make 13 blocks.

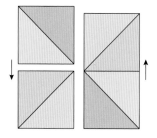

Make 13.

Piecing the Border Blocks

1. Repeat Piecing the Pinwheel Blocks, Steps 1 and 2 (page 11), using the 5⅜″ yellow squares and the remaining 5⅜″ pink squares. Make 96 half-square triangle units.

Make 96.

2. Arrange and sew 4 half-square triangle units as shown. Press. Make 24 blocks.

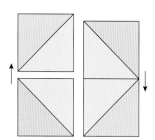

Make 24.

Assembling the Quilt

1. Refer to the quilt assembly diagram. Lay out the Cat blocks, Pinwheel blocks, and border blocks in 7 horizontal rows.

2. Sew the blocks into rows. Press.

3. Sew the rows together. Press the seams in one direction.

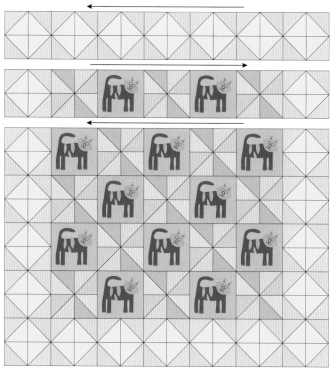

Quilt assembly diagram

Quilting and Binding

Refer to Basic Quiltmaking Instructions (pages 44–48) as needed to finish your quilt.

1. Divide the backing fabric in half selvage to selvage, reseam, and trim to make a 71″ × 71″ backing. Layer the quilt top, batting, and backing. Baste the three layers.

2. Quilt as desired.

3. Make binding using the 3″-wide pink #1 strips and finish the edges of the quilt.

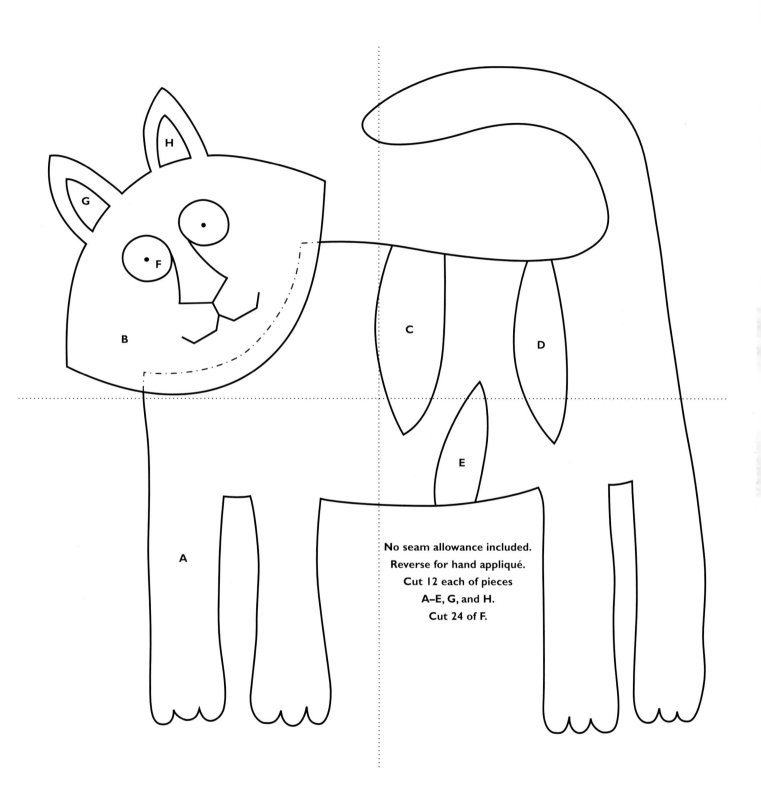

No seam allowance included.
Reverse for hand appliqué.
Cut 12 each of pieces
A–E, G, and H.
Cut 24 of F.

Party Fish

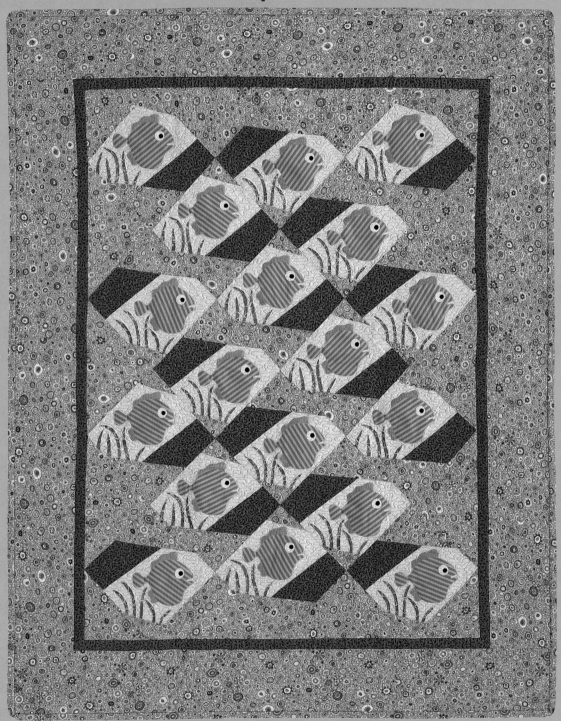

PARTY FISH

DESIGNED AND MADE BY CAROL BURNISTON,

MACHINE QUILTED BY JANET MURDOCK.

FINISHED QUILT: **52$\frac{1}{4}$" × 65"**

FINISHED BLOCK: **9" SQUARE**

Materials You'll Need

4¾ yards orange dotted print for blocks, side and corner
    setting triangles, outer border, and binding

1⅔ yards lime green print for blocks

1⅜ yards purple print for blocks and inner border

2 yards blue stripe for fish appliqués

⅜ yard hot pink print for fish appliqués

⅛ yard yellow print for fish appliqués

⅛ yard black solid or subtle print for fish appliqués

¾ yard green print for sea grass appliqués

3⅝ yards fabric for backing

61″ × 73″ piece of batting

7 yards lightweight 22″-wide fusible web

Thread to match appliqués

 ## Cutting the Fabric

Cut strips from the crosswise grain of the fabric.

> **note**
>
> *The side and corner setting triangles are cut
> slightly oversized. They will be trimmed after the
> quilt center is assembled. Patterns for A–D are
> on pages 17–18. Refer to Making Templates on
> page 44 for guidance as needed.*

From the orange dotted print, cut:

3 squares, 14¾″ × 14¾″; cut in half twice diagonally to
    make 12 quarter-square triangles (You will have 2
    leftover triangles.)

2 squares, 8″ × 8″; cut in half once diagonally to make 4
    half-square triangles

6 strips, 6½″ × 40″

7 strips, 3″ × 40″

18 A

18 D

From the lime green print, cut:

18 B

From the purple print, cut:

18 C

5 strips, 1½″ × 40″

 ## Piecing the Blocks

You need 18 pieced blocks. These are the background
blocks for the fish appliqués.

Lay out pieces A–D. Sew piece A to B. Press. Sew piece
C to the unit. Press. Sew piece D to the unit. Press. Make
18 blocks.

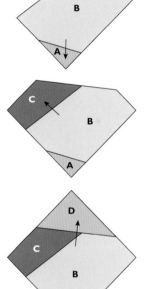

Make 18.

 ## Appliquéing the Fish

You need 18 appliquéd blocks: 9 each of Block 1 and
Block 2. Refer to Fusible Appliqué on page 45.

1. Use the patterns on page 17 to trace and cut 18 E
from the blue stripe, 18 each of F and G from the hot
pink print; 18 H from the yellow print, 18 I from the black
solid or print; and 9 each of J–S from the green print.

2. Refer to the appliqué placement diagrams below, noting the orientation of the pieces on the background blocks. Position 1 each of pieces E–I on each 9½″ pieced block. Position pieces J–S as shown. Fuse in place. Make 9 of each block.

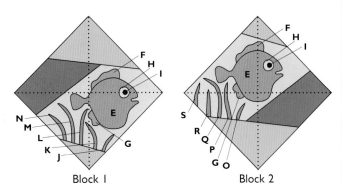

Block 1   Block 2

Appliqué placement diagrams
Make 9 of each block.

3. Finish the edges of the appliqués with matching-colored thread and a machine blanket stitch.

Assembling the Quilt

1. Refer to the quilt assembly diagram. Lay out the Fish blocks and the orange dotted side setting (quarter-square) triangles in 6 diagonal rows. Note that Block 1 and Block 2 make up alternating rows.

2. Sew the blocks into diagonal rows. Press.

3. Sew the rows together. Press the seams in one direction.

4. Sew the corner setting (half-square) triangles to the quilt. Press. Carefully trim the quilt to measure 38¾″ × 51½″.

5. Refer to Adding Borders on page 46. Sew the 1½″-wide purple strips end-to-end to make one continuous border strip. From this strip, cut 2 strips 1½″ × 51½″ for the side borders and 2 strips 1½″ × 40¾″ for the top and bottom borders.

6. Sew the 1½″ × 51½″ strips to the sides of the quilt. Press the seams toward the border strips. Sew the 1½″ × 40¾″ strips to the top and bottom of the quilt. Press.

7. Piece, measure, cut, and sew the 6½″-wide orange dotted borders to the quilt. Press the seams toward the purple borders.

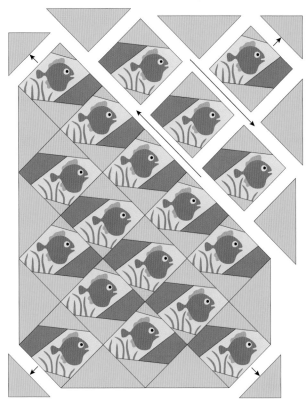

Quilt assembly diagram

Quilting and Binding

Refer to Basic Quiltmaking Instructions (pages 44–48) as needed to finish your quilt.

1. Divide the backing fabric in half selvage to selvage, reseam, and trim to make a 61″ × 73″ backing. Layer the quilt top, batting, and backing. Baste the three layers.

2. Quilt as desired.

3. Make binding using the 3″-wide orange dotted strips and finish the edges of the quilt.

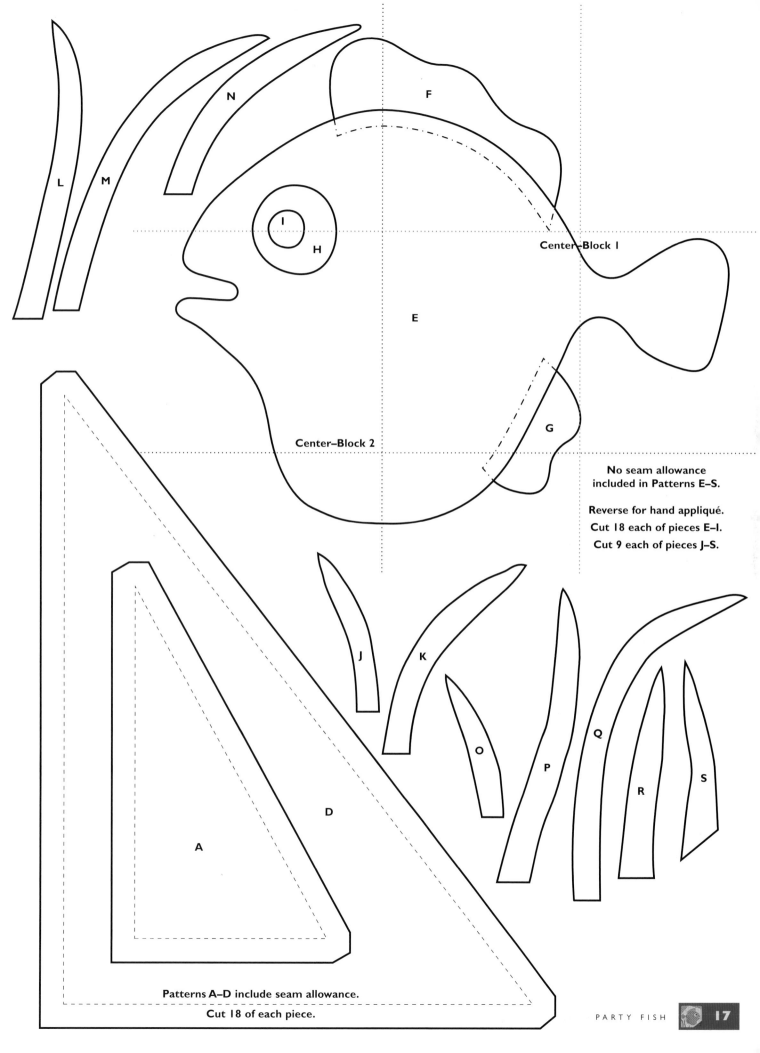

N

L M

F

I
H

Center–Block 1

E

Center–Block 2

G

No seam allowance
included in Patterns E–S.

Reverse for hand appliqué.
Cut 18 each of pieces E–I.
Cut 9 each of pieces J–S.

J K

D

O P Q R S

A

Patterns A–D include seam allowance.
Cut 18 of each piece.

B

C

Patterns B–C include seam allowance.

Cut 18 of each piece.

Strawberries on Parade

STRAWBERRIES ON PARADE
DESIGNED AND MADE BY CAROL BURNISTON,
MACHINE QUILTED BY JANET MURDOCK.
FINISHED QUILT: **58″** × **70″**
FINISHED BLOCK: **6″ SQUARE**

Materials You'll Need

3¼ yards bright white print or solid for appliqué background and pieced blocks

2⅛ yards medium green print or solid for pieced blocks and binding

2⅓ yards dark green print for pieced blocks and border

1 yard red print for strawberry appliqués

⅔ yard green print or solid for strawberry appliqués

4 yards fabric for backing

66″ × 78″ piece of batting

3¾ yards lightweight 22″-wide fusible web

Thread to match appliqués

 # Cutting the Fabric

Cut strips from the crosswise grain of the fabric.

From the bright white print or solid, cut:

32 squares, 6½″ × 6½″

4 strips, 4½″ × 40″

10 strips, 2½″ × 40″

6 strips, 1½″ × 40″

From the medium green print or solid, cut:

5 strips, 2½″ × 40″

18 strips, 1½″ × 40″

7 strips, 3″ × 40″

From the dark green print, cut:

15 strips, 2½″ × 40″; set aside 7 strips for border

4 strips, 1½″ × 40″

3 strips, 6½″ × 40″; crosscut into 18 squares, 6½″ × 6½″

3 strips, 6½″ × 40″; crosscut into 18 rectangles, 6½″ × 2½″

 # Appliquéing the Strawberry Blocks

You need 32 appliquéd blocks. Refer to Fusible Appliqué on page 45.

1. Use the patterns on page 22 to trace and cut 32 A from the red print and 32 B from the green print or solid.

2. Refer to the appliqué placement diagram below. Position 1 A and 1 B on each 6½″ bright white square. Fuse in place. Make 32 blocks.

3. Finish the edges of the appliqués with matching-colored thread and a machine blanket stitch.

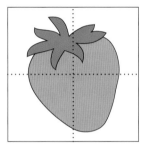

Appliqué placement diagram
Make 32 blocks.

 # Piecing the Blocks

You need 49 pieced blocks: 17 of Block 1, 14 of Block 2, and 18 of Block 3.

Block 1

1. Sew a 4½″ × 40″ bright white strip between two 1½″ × 40″ medium green strips. Press. Make 4 strip sets. Cut 80 segments, each 1½″ wide. Label them A and set 46 aside for Blocks 2 and 3.

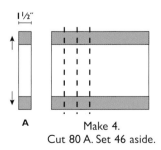

1½″

A

Make 4.
Cut 80 A. Set 46 aside.

2. Sew a 2½″ × 40″ bright white strip, two 1½″ × 40″ medium green strips, and two 1½″ × 40″ bright white strips together. Press. Make 2 strip sets. Cut 34 segments, each 1½″ wide. Label them B.

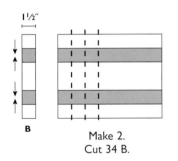

B
Make 2.
Cut 34 B.

3. Sew a 2½″ × 40″ medium green strip between two 2½″ × 40″ bright white strips. Press. Make 2 strip sets. Cut 17 segments, each 2½″ wide. Label them C.

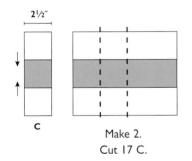

C
Make 2.
Cut 17 C.

4. Sew together 1 C segment, 2 B segments, and 2 A segments. Press. Make 17 and label them Block 1.

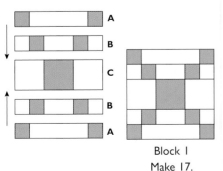

A
B
C
B
A

Block 1
Make 17.

Block 2

1. Sew together a 2½″ × 40″ bright white strip, two 1½″ × 40″ medium green strips, a 1½″ × 40″ dark green strip, and a 1½″ × 40″ bright white strip. Press. Make 2 strip sets. Cut 28 segments, each 1½″ wide. Label them D.

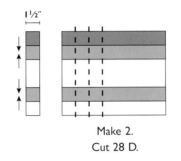

Make 2.
Cut 28 D.

2. Sew a 2½″ × 40″ medium green strip between a 2½″ × 40″ bright white strip and a 2½″ × 40″ dark green strip. Press. Cut 14 segments, each 2½″ wide. Label them E.

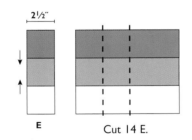

E
Cut 14 E.

3. Sew together 1 E segment, 2 D segments, and 2 A segments. Press. Make 14 and label them Block 2.

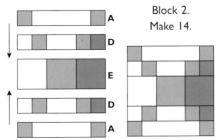

A
D
E
D
A

Block 2.
Make 14.

Block 3

1. Sew together a 2½″ × 40″ bright white strip, two 1½″ × 40″ medium green strips, and two 1½″ × 40″ dark green strips. Press. Cut 18 segments, each 1½″ wide. Label them F.

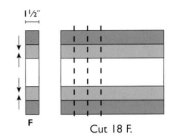

F
Cut 18 F.

2. Sew a 2½″ × 40″ medium green strip between two 2½″ × 40″ dark green strips. Press. Make 2 strip sets. Cut 18 segments, each 2½″ wide. Label them G.

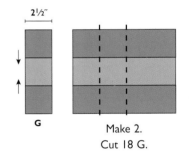

G
Make 2.
Cut 18 G.

3. Sew together 1 each of segments G, F, A, and a 2½″ × 6½″ dark green print strip. Press. Make 18 and label them Block 3.

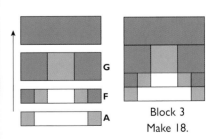

G
F
A

Block 3
Make 18.

Assembling the Quilt

1. Refer to the quilt assembly diagram. Lay out the Strawberry blocks; Blocks 1, 2, and 3; and the 6½" dark green squares in 11 horizontal rows.

2. Sew the blocks into rows. Press.

3. Sew the rows together. Press the seams in one direction. The quilt should measure 54½" × 66½".

4. Refer to Adding Borders on page 46. Sew the remaining 2½"-wide dark green strips end-to-end to make one continuous border strip. From this strip, cut 2 strips 2½" × 66½" for the side borders and 2 strips 2½" × 58½" for the top and bottom borders.

5. Sew the 2½" × 66½" strips to the sides of the quilt. Press the seams toward the border strips. Sew the 2½" × 58½" strips to the top and bottom of the quilt. Press.

Quilting and Binding

Refer to Basic Quiltmaking Instructions (pages 44–48) as needed to finish your quilt.

1. Divide the backing fabric in half selvage to selvage, reseam, and trim to make a 66" × 78" backing. Layer the quilt top, batting, and backing. Baste the three layers.

2. Quilt as desired.

3. Make binding using the 3"-wide medium green strips and finish the edges of the quilt.

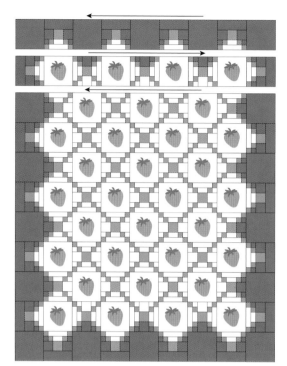

Quilt assembly diagram

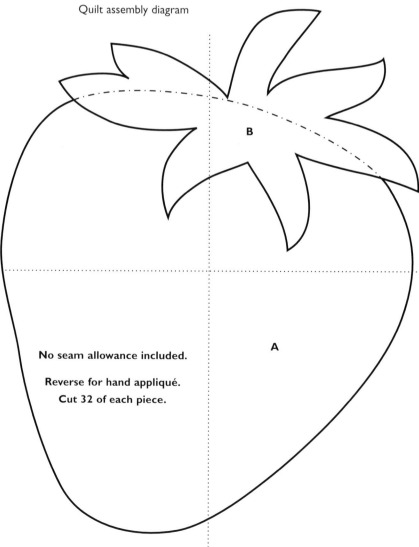

No seam allowance included.

Reverse for hand appliqué.
Cut 32 of each piece.

B

A

Outside the Box

OUTSIDE THE BOX

DESIGNED AND MADE BY CAROL BURNISTON,
MACHINE QUILTED BY JANET MURDOCK.
FINISHED QUILT: **73$\frac{1}{2}$″ × 94$\frac{1}{2}$″**
FINISHED BLOCK: **10$\frac{1}{2}$″ SQUARE**

⬚ Materials You'll Need

2⅜ yards total of assorted blue prints for blocks

3¼ yards red print for blocks

4⅓ yards yellow print for blocks

6 yards fabric for backing

82″ × 103″ piece of batting

⬚ Cutting the Fabric

Cut strips from the crosswise grain of the fabric.
From the assorted blue prints, cut:

734 squares, 2″ × 2″

From the red print, cut:

42 strips, 2″ × 40″; crosscut into:

    140 rectangles, 2″ × 8″

    72 rectangles, 2″ × 5″

    72 squares, 2″ × 2″

3 strips, 5″ × 40″; crosscut into 17 squares, 5″ × 5″

From the yellow print, cut:

9 strips, 3″ × 40″

52 strips, 2″ × 40″; crosscut into:

    112 rectangles, 2″ × 8″

    180 rectangles, 2″ × 5″

    112 squares, 2″ × 2″

⬚ Piecing the Blocks

You need 63 pieced blocks: 17 of Block 1, 18 of Block 2, and 28 of Block 3.

Block 1

1. Lay out one 5″ red square, four 2″ × 5″ yellow rectangles, and four 2″ assorted blue squares. Sew the squares and rectangles into rows. Press. Sew the rows together. Press. Make 17.

Make 17.

2. Lay out 1 unit from Step 1, four 2″ × 8″ red rectangles, and four 2″ assorted blue squares. Sew the unit, rectangles, and squares into rows. Press. Sew the rows together. Press. Make 17 and label them Block 1.

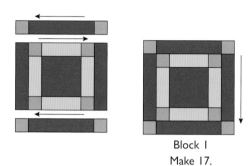

Block 1
Make 17.

Block 2

1. Lay out five 2″ assorted blue squares and four 2″ red squares. Sew the squares into rows. Press. Sew the rows together. Press. Make 18.

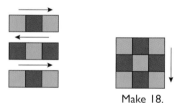

Make 18.

2. Lay out 1 unit from Step 1, four 2″ × 5″ red rectangles, and four 2″ assorted blue squares. Sew the unit, rectangles, and squares into rows. Press. Sew the rows together. Press. Make 18.

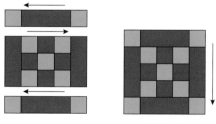

Make 18.

3. Lay out 1 unit from Step 2, four 2″ × 8″ red rectangles, and four 2″ assorted blue squares. Sew the unit, rectangles, and squares into rows. Press. Sew the rows together. Press. Make 18 and label them Block 2.

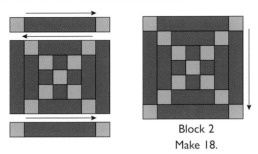

Block 2
Make 18.

Block 3

1. Lay out five 2″ assorted blue squares and four 2″ yellow squares. Sew the squares into rows. Press. Sew the rows together. Press. Make 28.

Make 28.

2. Lay out 1 unit from Step 1, four 2″ × 5″ yellow rectangles, and four 2″ assorted blue squares. Sew the unit, rectangles, and squares into rows. Press. Sew the rows together. Press. Make 28.

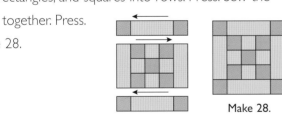

Make 28.

3. Lay out 1 unit from Step 2, four 2″ × 8″ yellow rectangles, and four 2″ assorted blue squares. Sew the unit, rectangles, and squares into rows. Press. Sew the rows together. Press. Make 28 and label them Block 3.

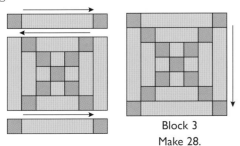

Block 3
Make 28.

Assembling the Quilt

1. Refer to the quilt assembly diagram. Lay out Blocks 1, 2, and 3 in 9 horizontal rows.

2. Sew the blocks into rows. Press.

3. Sew the rows together. Press the seams in one direction.

Quilt assembly diagram

Quilting and Binding

Refer to Basic Quiltmaking Instructions (pages 44–48) as needed to finish your quilt.

1. Divide the backing fabric in half selvage to selvage, reseam, and trim to make an 82″ × 103″ backing. Layer the quilt top, batting, and backing. Baste the three layers.

2. Quilt as desired.

3. Make binding using the 3″-wide yellow strips and finish the edges of the quilt.

Hot Tamale Sunflowers

HOT TAMALE SUNFLOWERS
DESIGNED AND MADE BY CAROL BURNISTON,
MACHINE QUILTED BY JANET MURDOCK.
FINISHED QUILT: 66½″ × 72″
FINISHED BLOCK: 8½″X 12½″

Materials You'll Need

2¼ yards light blue print for appliqué background

1¾ yards purple print for border

1 yard orange print for binding

⅓ yard each of 15–20 assorted colorful prints for flower
   appliqués and sashing

¼ yard each of 8–10 assorted green prints for stem and
   leaf appliqués and sashing

4⅜ yards fabric for backing

75″ × 80″ piece of batting

7 yards lightweight 22″-wide fusible web

Thread to match appliqués

Cutting the Fabric

Cut strips from the crosswise grain of the fabric.

From the light blue print, cut:

7 strips, 9″ × 40″; crosscut into 20 blocks, 9″ × 13″

From the purple print, cut:

7 strips, 6½″ × 40″

From the orange print, cut:

8 strips, 3″ × 40″

From the assorted colorful and green print fabrics, cut:

48 strips, 1½″ × 13″

50 strips, 1½″ × 11″

20 squares, 1½″ × 1½″

Appliquéing the Sunflower Blocks

You need 20 appliquéd blocks. Refer to Fusible Appliqué on page 45.

1. Use the patterns on pages 28–29 to trace and cut 20 of each piece A–D from the assorted colorful prints and 20 of each piece E–G from the assorted green prints.

2. Refer to the appliqué placement diagram below. Position 1 each of A–G on each 9″ × 13″ light blue block. Fuse in place. Make 20 blocks.

3. Finish the edges of the appliqués with matching-colored thread and a machine blanket stitch.

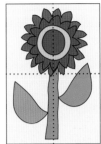

Appliqué placement diagram
Make 20 blocks.

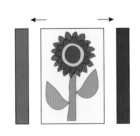 Adding the Sashing

Sew a different-colored 1½″ × 13″ print strip to opposite sides of each block. Press. Sew a different-colored 1½″ × 11″ strip to the top and bottom of each block. Press.

Assembling the Quilt

1. Refer to the quilt assembly diagram on page 29. Lay out the sashed Sunflower blocks in four horizontal rows, turning the blocks as shown.

2. Sew the blocks into rows. Press.

3. Sew the rows together. Press the seams in one direction.

4. Sew 5 different 1½″ × 11″ print strips together end-to-end to make a sashing strip. Make 2. Press the seams in one direction. Sew the sashing strips to the top and bottom of the quilt. Press.

5. Sew together 10 different 1½" print squares and 4 different 1½" × 13" strips to make a sashing strip. Make 2. Press. Sew the strips to the sides of the quilt. Press. The quilt should measure 55" × 60½".

6. Refer to Adding Borders on page 46. Sew the 6½"-wide purple strips end-to-end to make one continuous border strip. From this strip, cut 2 strips 6½" × 60½" for the side borders and 2 strips 6½" × 67" for the top and bottom borders.

7. Sew the 6½" × 60½" strips to the sides of the quilt. Press the seams toward the border strips. Sew the 6½" × 67" strips to the top and bottom of the quilt. Press.

Make 2.

![sunflower icon] Quilting and Binding

Refer to Basic Quiltmaking Instructions (pages 44–48) as needed to finish your quilt.

1. Divide the backing fabric in half selvage to selvage, reseam, and trim to make a 75″ × 80″ backing. Layer the quilt top, batting, and backing. Baste the three layers.

2. Quilt as desired.

3. Make binding using the 3″-wide orange print strips and finish the edges of the quilt.

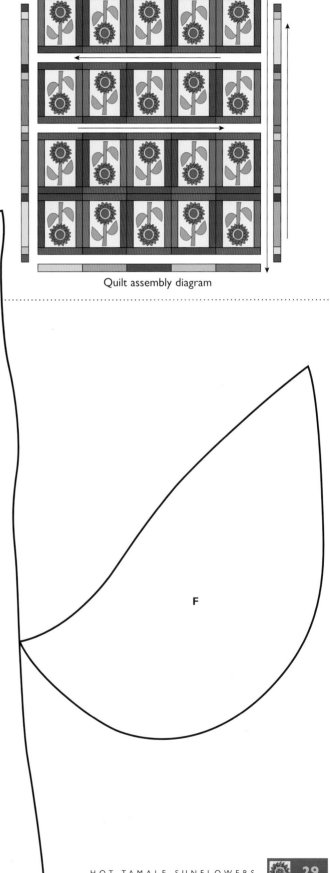

Quilt assembly diagram

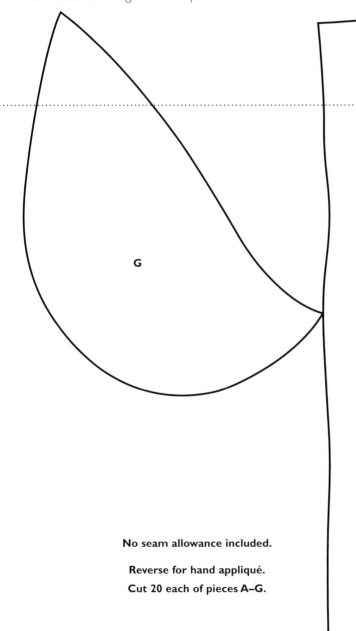

G

E

F

No seam allowance included.

Reverse for hand appliqué.

Cut 20 each of pieces A–G.

Sheep in Dreamland

SHEEP IN DREAMLAND
DESIGNED AND MADE BY CAROL BURNISTON,
MACHINE QUILTED BY JANET MURDOCK.
FINISHED QUILT: **56″ × 72″**
FINISHED BLOCK: **8″ SQUARE**

Materials You'll Need

2⅝ yards blue print for appliqué background

2¾ yards aqua marbled print for pinwheel appliqués and border

3⅔ yards pink marbled print for sheep appliqués, border scallops, and binding

⅞ yard black print or solid for sheep appliqués

Scraps of yellow print for sheep appliqués

3⅞ yards fabric for backing

64″ × 80″ piece of batting

9 yards lightweight 22″-wide fusible web

Thread to match appliqués

Yellow and black embroidery floss

 ## Cutting the Fabric

Cut strips from the crosswise grain of the fabric.

From the blue print, cut:

9 strips, 8½″ × 40″; crosscut into 35 squares, 8½″ × 8½″

From the aqua marbled print, cut:

6 strips, 8½″ × 40″

From the pink marbled print, cut:

7 strips, 3″ × 40″

Appliquéing the Sheep and Pinwheel Blocks

You need 35 appliquéd blocks: 18 Sheep blocks and 17 Pinwheel blocks. Refer to Fusible Appliqué on page 45.

1. Use the patterns on pages 32–33 to trace and cut 18 A from the pink print; 18 B from the black print or solid; 72 C from the black print or solid; 18 each of D–F from the yellow prints; and 68 G from the aqua print.

2. Use pattern B to trace the sheep's face on each B piece.

3. Refer to the quilt photo on page 30 for sheep placement ideas. Position 1 each of A and B, 4 C, and 1 each of D–F on a 8½″ blue print block, changing the positions of the A, B, and C pieces. Fuse in place. Make 18 blocks.

4. Refer to the pinwheel appliqué placement diagram below. Position 4 G on each remaining 8½″ blue print block. Fuse in place. Make 17 blocks.

5. Refer to Embroidery Stitches on page 46. Use 2 strands of yellow embroidery floss and a backstitch to embroider each sheep's mouth. Use black embroidery floss to make a French knot in the center of each eye.

6. Finish the edges of the appliqués with matching-colored thread and a machine blanket stitch.

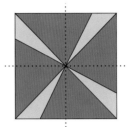

Appliqué placement diagram
Make 17 blocks.

Assembling the Quilt

1. Refer to the quilt assembly diagram on page 32. Lay out the Sheep and Pinwheel blocks in 7 horizontal rows, alternating the blocks as shown.

2. Sew the blocks into rows. Press.

3. Sew the rows together. Press the seams in one direction. The quilt should measure 40½″ × 56½″.

Appliquéing and Adding the Border

1. Sew the 8½″-wide aqua marbled strips end-to-end to make one continuous border strip. From this strip, cut 4 strips 8½″ × 56½″.

2. Refer to Fusible Appliqué on page 45. Use the patterns on page 33 to trace and cut 48 H and 4 I from the pink print.

3. Position 7 H along both long edges of a 8½″ × 56½″ aqua strip to make a side border. Fuse in place. Make 2. Position 10 H and 2 I on each remaining strip to make the top and bottom borders.

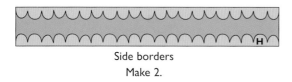

Side borders
Make 2.

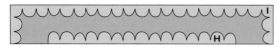

Top and bottom borders
Make 2.

4. Finish the edges of the appliqués with matching-colored thread and a machine blanket stitch.

5. Refer to Adding Borders on page 46. Sew the side borders from Step 3 to the quilt. Press the seams toward the border strips. Sew the top and bottom borders to the quilt. Press.

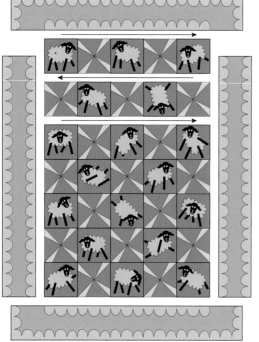

Quilt assembly diagram

Quilting and Binding

Refer to Basic Quiltmaking Instructions (pages 44–48) as needed to finish your quilt.

1. Divide the backing fabric in half selvage to selvage, reseam, and trim to make a 64″ × 80″ backing. Layer the quilt top, batting, and backing. Baste the three layers.

2. Quilt as desired.

3. Make binding using the 3″-wide marbled pink strips and finish the edges of the quilt.

No seam allowance included.
Reverse for hand appliqué.
Cut 18 of each piece.

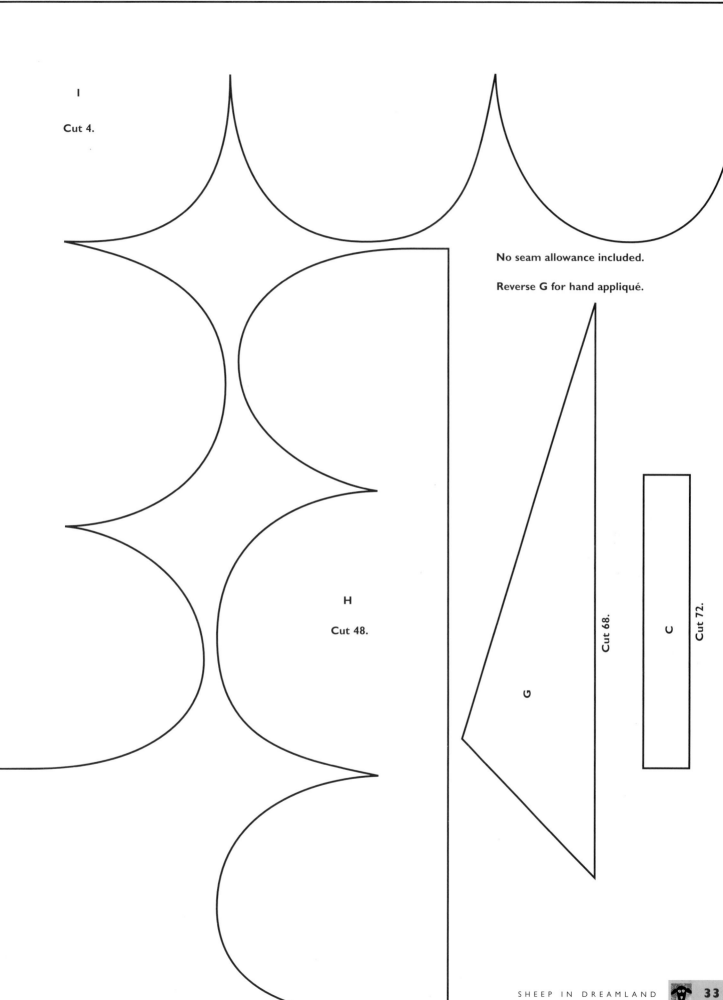

I

Cut 4.

No seam allowance included.

Reverse G for hand appliqué.

H

Cut 48.

Cut 68.

G

C

Cut 72.

Liberty

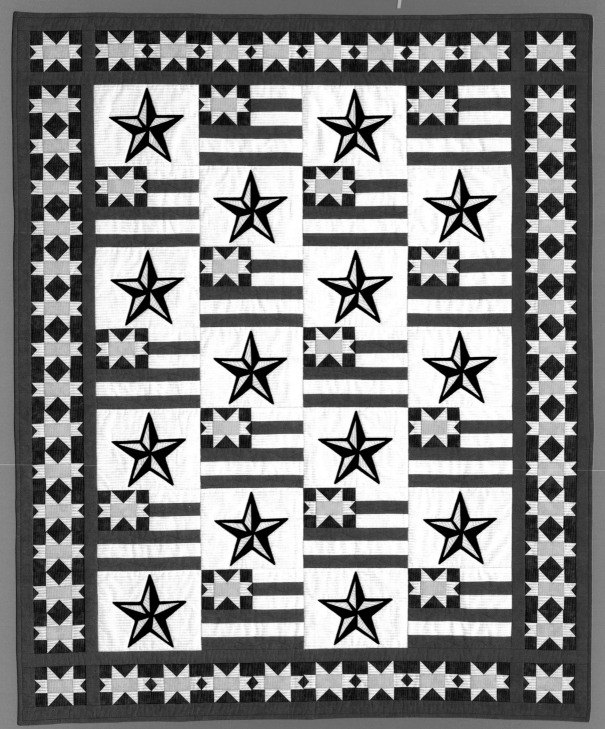

LIBERTY
DESIGNED AND MADE BY CAROL BURNISTON,
MACHINE QUILTED BY JANET MURDOCK.
FINISHED QUILT: **44″ × 52″**
FINISHED BLOCK: **6″ × 8″**

Materials You'll Need

2⅔ yards bright white stripe for Flag blocks, large Star
   block background, and small star appliqués
1⅛ yards blue solid or marbled print for small Star block
   backgrounds
⅜ yard yellow solid for small star appliqués
1 yard bright white print for large star appliqués
1 yard black print for large star appliqués
1⅔ yards red solid or subtle print for Flag blocks,
   borders, and binding
3¼ yards fabric for backing
52″ × 60″ piece of batting
6¾ yards lightweight 22″-wide fusible web
Thread to match appliqués

Cutting the Fabrics

Cut strips from the crosswise grain of the fabric.
From the bright white stripe, cut:
4 strips, 6½″ × 40″; crosscut into 14 rectangles,
   6½″ × 8½″
8 strips, 1½″ × 40″; crosscut into:
   14 strips, 1½″ × 8½″
   28 rectangles, 1½″ × 4½″
From the red subtle print or solid, cut:
6 strips, 3″ × 40″
19 strips, 1½″ × 40″; set aside 9 strips for borders.
Cross cut the remaining strips into:
   28 strips, 1½″ × 8½″
   14 rectangles, 1½″ × 4½″
   8 rectangles, 1½″ × 3½″
From the blue solid or marbled print, cut:
8 strips, 3½″ × 40″; crosscut into 62 rectangles, 3½″ × 4½″

Appliquéing the Large and Small Star Blocks

**You need 76 appliquéd blocks: 14 large Star blocks and 62
small Star blocks. Refer to Fusible Appliqué on page 45.**
1. Use the patterns on page 37 to trace and cut 14 A
from the black print; 14 each of B–F from the bright
white print; 62 G from the bright white stripe; and 62 H
from the yellow solid.
2. Refer to the large star appliqué placement diagram
below. Position 1 each of A–F on each 6½″ × 8½″ bright
white stripe rectangle. Fuse in place. Make 14 blocks.
3. Refer to the small star appliqué placement diagram.
Position 1 each of G and H on each 3½″ × 4½″ blue solid
or marbled print rectangle. Fuse in place. Make 62 blocks.
4. Finish the edges of the appliqués with matching-
colored thread and a machine blanket stitch.

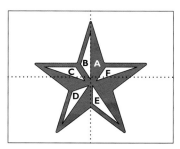

Large star appliqué placement diagram
Make 14 blocks.

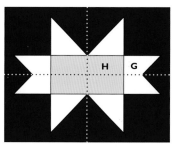

Small star appliqué placement diagram
Make 62 blocks.

Piecing the Flag Blocks

1. Sew a 1½″ × 4½″ red subtle print or solid rectangle between two 1½″ × 4½″ bright white stripe rectangles. Press. Make 14.

Make 14.

2. Sew a 1½″ × 8½″ bright white stripe rectangle between two 1½″ × 8½″ red subtle print or solid strips. Press. Make 14.

Make 14.

3. Sew a small Star block and 1 unit each from Steps 1 and 2 together. Press. Make 14 Flag blocks.

Flag block
Make 14.

Assembling the Quilt

1. Refer to the quilt assembly diagram. Lay out the large Star and Flag blocks in 7 horizontal rows, alternating the blocks as shown.

2. Sew the blocks into rows. Press.

3. Sew the rows together. Press the seams in one direction. The quilt should measure 32½″ × 42½″.

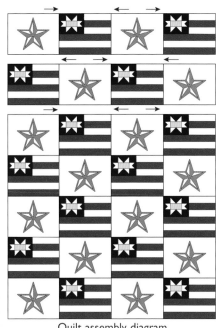

Quilt assembly diagram

Piecing and Adding the Border

1. Refer to Adding Borders on page 46. Sew the 9 remaining 1½″-wide red subtle print or solid strips end-to-end to make one continuous border strip. From this strip, cut 4 strips, 1½″ × 42½″ and 4 strips, 1½″ × 44½″.

2. Lay out and sew 14 small Star blocks in a row to make a side border as shown. Press. Sew the row between two 1½″ × 42½″ red strips. Press. Make 2.

Side border
Make 2.

Top and bottom border
Make 2.

3. Lay out and sew 10 small Star blocks and four 1½″ × 3½″ red subtle print or solid rectangles in a row to make a top or bottom border as shown above. Press. Sew the row between two 1½″ × 44½″ red strips. Press. Make 2.

4. Refer to the quilt photo on page 34. Sew the borders from Step 2 to the sides of the quilt. Press the seams toward the red strips. Sew the borders from Step 3 to the top and bottom of the quilt. Press.

✶ Quilting and Binding

Refer to Basic Quiltmaking Instructions (pages 44–48) as needed to finish your quilt.

1. Divide the backing fabric in half selvage to selvage, reseam, and trim to make a 52″ × 60″ backing. Layer the quilt top, batting, and backing. Baste the three layers.

2. Quilt as desired.

3. Make binding using the 3″-wide red strips and finish the edges of the quilt.

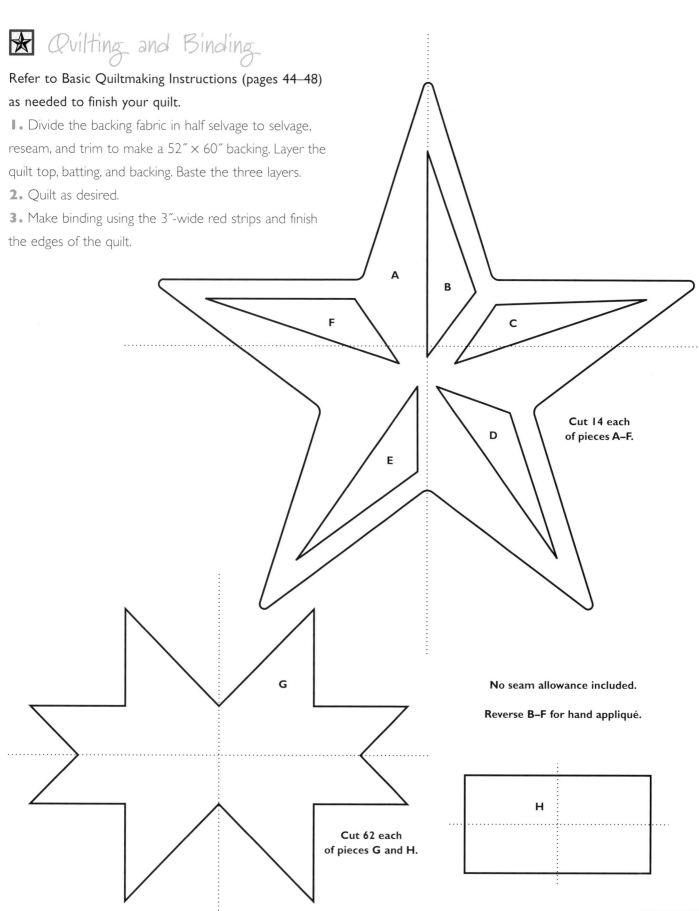

Cut 14 each of pieces **A–F.**

No seam allowance included.

Reverse **B–F** for hand appliqué.

Cut 62 each of pieces **G** and **H.**

Quack Quack

QUACK QUACK
DESIGNED AND MADE BY CAROL BURNISTON,
MACHINE QUILTED BY JANET MURDOCK.
FINISHED QUILT: **56"** × **60"**

Materials You'll Need

2⅓ yards light print for blocks

2 yards red print for blocks and binding

2 yards purple print for border

1 yard yellow print for duck appliqués

¼ yard orange solid or subtle print for duck appliqués

Scraps of black solid for duck appliqués

⅝ yard lime green print for wavy appliqués

3⅞ yards fabric for backing

64″ × 68″ piece of batting

3¾ yards lightweight 22″-wide fusible web

Thread to match appliqués

Cutting the Fabric

Cut strips from the crosswise grain of the fabric.

From the light print, cut:

28 strips, 2½″ × 40″; crosscut into 220 rectangles, 2½″ × 4½″

From the red print, cut:

14 strips, 2½″ × 40″; crosscut into 220 squares, 2½″ × 2½″

7 strips, 3″ × 40″

From the purple print, cut:

6 strips, 8½″ × 40″

Assembling the Quilt

1. Mark a diagonal line on the wrong side of each 2½″ red square. Align a marked square, right sides together, with one end of each 2½″ × 4½″ light rectangle. Sew on the drawn line. Cut away the excess fabric, leaving a ¼″ seam allowance. Press. Make 220.

Make 220.

2. Lay out 10 units from Step 1. Sew the units together to make a row. Press. Make 22 rows.

Make 22.

3. Refer to the quilt photo on page 38 and the diagram below. Lay out the 22 rows, alternating the direction of the red triangles from row to row. Sew the rows together. Press. The quilt should measure 40½″ × 44½″.

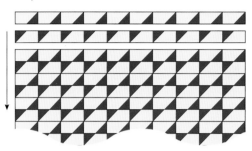

4. Refer to Adding Borders on page 46. Sew the 8½″-wide purple print strips end-to-end to make one continuous border strip. From this strip, cut 2 strips, 8½″ × 44½″ and 2 strips, 8½″ × 56½″.

5. Sew the 8½″ × 44½″ strips to the sides of the quilt. Press the seams toward the border strips. Sew the 8½″ × 56½″ strips to the top and bottom of the quilt. Press.

Appliquéing the Border

You need 24 waves, 4 large ducks, and 30 small ducks. Refer to Fusible Appliqué on page 45.

1. Use the patterns on page 40 to trace and cut 24 A from the lime green print; 30 B and 4 E from the orange solid or subtle print; 30 C and 4 F from the yellow print; and 30 D and 4 G from the black solid.

2. Refer to the quilt photo on page 38. Position 24 A pieces (6 on both sides, the top, and the bottom) 1″ from the quilt center on the purple print border. Fuse in place.

3. Refer to the quilt photo. Position 1 each of E, F, and G on each corner. Fuse in place.

4. Refer to the quilt photo. Position pieces B, C, and D to make 8 small ducks on each side border and 7 small ducks on the top and border, spacing them as shown. (The ducks should appear to be riding the waves.) Fuse in place.

5. Finish the edges of the appliqués with matching-colored thread and a machine blanket stitch.

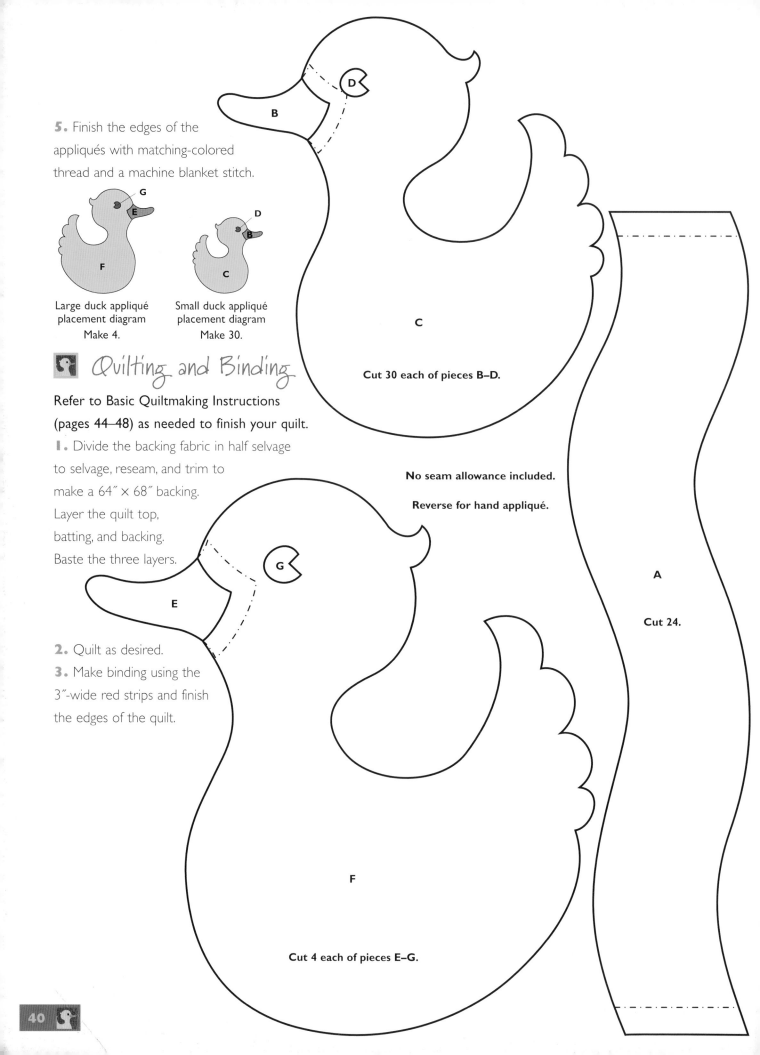

Large duck appliqué
placement diagram
Make 4.

Small duck appliqué
placement diagram
Make 30.

Quilting and Binding

Refer to Basic Quiltmaking Instructions (pages 44–48) as needed to finish your quilt.

1. Divide the backing fabric in half selvage to selvage, reseam, and trim to make a 64″ × 68″ backing. Layer the quilt top, batting, and backing. Baste the three layers.

2. Quilt as desired.

3. Make binding using the 3″-wide red strips and finish the edges of the quilt.

Cut 30 each of pieces B–D.

No seam allowance included.

Reverse for hand appliqué.

A

Cut 24.

Cut 4 each of pieces E–G.

Flowers on the Vine

FLOWERS ON THE VINE
DESIGNED AND MADE BY CAROL BURNISTON,
MACHINE QUILTED BY JANET MURDOCK.
FINISHED QUILT: **46˝ × 60½˝**
FINISHED BLOCK: **12˝ SQUARE**

Materials You'll Need

1¾ yards white print for block background

2⅛ yards red stripe for sashing and binding*

½ yard yellow subtle print for corner stones

1¼ yards blue print for blocks and corner stones

¾ yard total assorted red prints for flower appliqués

⅝ yard total assorted blue prints for flower appliqués

½ yard total assorted yellow prints for flower appliqués

1¼ yards total assorted green prints for leaf and stem
appliqués

3¼ yards fabric for backing

54″ × 69″ piece of batting

6⅝ yards lightweight 22″-wide fusible web

Thread to match appliqués

* *Based on a stripe that runs parallel to the selvage.*

Cutting the Fabric

Cut strips from the crosswise grain of the fabric.

From the white print, cut:

4 strips, 10½″ × 40″; crosscut into 12 squares, 10½″ × 10½″

From the red stripe, cut:

5 strips, 5¼″ × 40″; crosscut into 62 rectangles, 3″ × 5¼″
(When crosscutting, stripes run parallel to the longer
measurement.)

3 strips, 3″ × 40″; crosscut into 31 squares, 3″ × 3″

6 strips, 3″ × 40″

From the yellow subtle print, cut:

2 strips, 3″ × 40″; crosscut into 20 squares, 3″ × 3″

From the blue print, cut:

16 strips, 1½″ × 40; crosscut into 24 strips, 1½″ × 10½″
and 24 strips, 1½″ × 12½″

4 strips, 1¾″ × 40″; crosscut into 80 squares, 1¾″ × 1¾″

Appliqueing the Blocks

**You need 12 appliquéd blocks. Refer to Fusible
Appliqué on page 45.**

1. Use the patterns on page 43 to trace and cut 36 each
of A and B and 72 each of C and D from the green prints;

12 E from the red prints; 12 F from the blue prints; and 12
G from the assorted yellow prints. Cut 12 A and 12 B in
half; label them AA and BB. You will have 24 short vines of
each (AA and BB) and 24 long vines of each (A and B).

2. Refer to the appliqué placement diagram below.
Position 2 each of A, AA, B, and BB; 6 each of C and D;
and 1 each of E, F, and G on each 10½″ white square.
Fuse in place. Make 12 blocks.

3. Finish the edges of
the appliqués with
matching-colored
thread and a machine
blanket stitch.

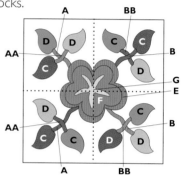

Appliqué placement diagram
Make 12 blocks.

4. Sew a 1½″ × 10½″ blue strip to opposite sides of
each block. Press. Sew a 1½″ × 12½″ blue strip to the
top and bottom of each block. Press.

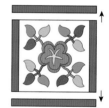

Making the Corner Stones and Sashing

1. Mark a diagonal line on the wrong side of each 1¾″
blue print square. Align a marked square, right sides
together, with opposite corners of each 3″ yellow subtle
print square. Sew on the drawn line. Cut away the
excess fabric, leaving a ¼″ seam allowance. Press. Repeat
to sew a 1¾″ blue square to the remaining corners. Trim
and press. Make 20.

Sew first,

**then
cut.**

Make 20.

2. Sew a 3″ × 5¼″ red stripe rectangle to opposite sides of each 3″ red stripe square. (Position the square so the stripes run from top to bottom.) Press. Make 31.

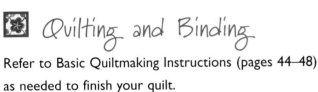

Make 31.

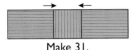 ## Assembling the Quilt

1. Refer to the quilt assembly diagram to the right. Lay out and sew 3 blocks and 4 sashing strips as shown. Sew the blocks and strips together. Press the seams toward the strips. Make 4 rows.

2. Lay out and sew 3 sashing strips and 4 corner stones. Sew the squares and strips together. Press the seams toward the strips. Make 5 rows.

3. Lay out the rows from Steps 1 and 2, alternating as shown. Sew the rows together. Press the seams in one direction.

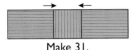 ## Quilting and Binding

Refer to Basic Quiltmaking Instructions (pages 44–48) as needed to finish your quilt.

1. Divide the backing fabric in half selvage to selvage, reseam, and trim to make a 54″ × 69″ backing. Layer the quilt top, batting, and backing. Baste the three layers.

2. Quilt as desired.

3. Make binding using the 3″-wide red stripe strips and finish the edges of the quilt.

Quilt assembly diagram

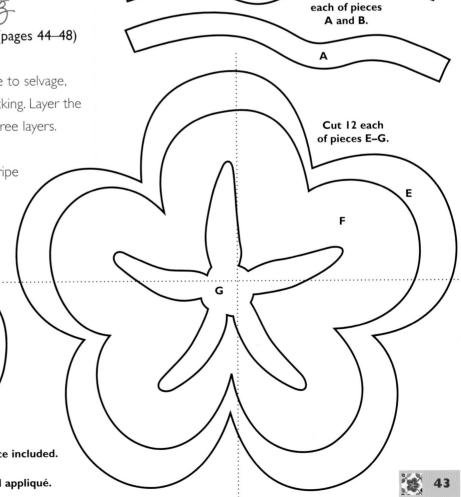

B

Cut 36 each of pieces A and B.

A

Cut 12 each of pieces E–G.

E

F

G

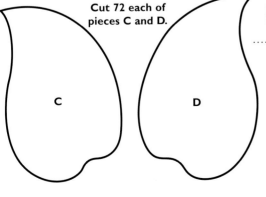

Cut 72 each of pieces C and D.

C

D

No seam allowance included.

Reverse for hand appliqué.

43

Basic Quiltmaking
INSTRUCTIONS

The following pages contain the basic information you need to complete the quilts in this book, as well as many other quilt projects you may choose to make. Yardage is based on 40″ wide fabric.

MAKING TEMPLATES

Party Fish (page 14) includes a few full-size pattern pieces that you may want to cut with templates. Look for clear, easy-to-cut template plastic at quilt shops or your favorite mail-order sources.

To make a template, place the plastic over each pattern and trace with a fine-point permanent marker. Do not add seam allowances; cut out the template directly on the drawn lines.

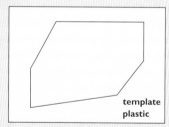

template plastic

Cut on drawn line.

MACHINE PIECING AND PRESSING

Use a ¼″-wide seam allowance for all piecing.

The illustrations that accompany step-by-step project instructions include pressing arrows to guide you. In general, you will press seams toward the darker fabric or in the direction that creates the least amount of bulk. Unless instructed otherwise, when sewing blocks into rows, press the seams in odd-numbered rows in one direction, and press the seams in even-numbered rows in

the opposite direction. This creates opposing (or "nesting") seams. Opposing seams are easier to match, and reduce bulkiness when the rows are joined.

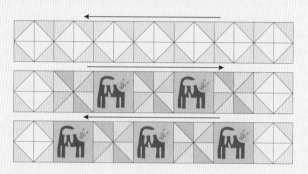

> **tip**
>
> *Press lightly in an up-and-down motion. Don't let your iron get too hot, and don't drag the iron across the fabric; both can distort the shapes and blocks.*

PREPARING FOR APPLIQUÉ

Lightly press each background block in half vertically, horizontally, and then diagonally to find the center of the block and to create placement guidelines for the appliqué shapes. Press carefully so you don't stretch the block.

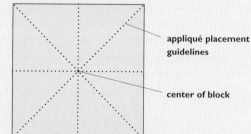

appliqué placement guidelines

center of block

FUSIBLE APPLIQUÉ

The appliqué patterns in this book are reversed for fusible appliqué. You can find fusible web at quilt and sewing shops. Be sure to get the lightweight type; it is difficult to sew through heavyweight fusible web. Instructions for these products vary depending upon the manufacturer, so read the product instructions before you begin.

You will find one or more appliqué placement diagrams with most projects to guide you in placing the appliqué shapes. Each pattern piece is identified by letter; appliqué the pieces in alphabetical order.

If you prefer hand appliqué, see the instructions in the next column to adapt the patterns for handwork.

1. Place the fusible web paper-side up over the pattern pieces. (If you prefer, use the pattern to create a plastic template. See page 44.) Use a pencil to trace the required number of each pattern piece onto the fusible web. Cut out the pieces ¼″ outside the traced lines.

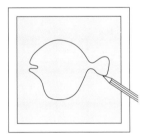

Trace the pattern or template onto the fusible web.

Cut out ¼" outside the line.

2. Follow the manufacturer's instructions to press the adhesive side of the fusible web to the wrong side of the appropriate appliqué fabrics. Allow to cool. Cut out the fabric shapes directly on the traced lines. Peel off the paper backing.

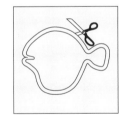

wrong side of fabric

Cut directly on the drawn line.

3. Refer to the quilt photo and/or appliqué placement diagram in the project instructions to arrange the fabric pieces on the appliqué background. Follow the manufacturer's instructions to fuse the appliqués to the background.

4. Use matching-colored thread to finish the raw edges of the appliqués with a machine blanket stitch. If you prefer, you can finish the edges with a hand blanket stitch or machine satin stitch instead.

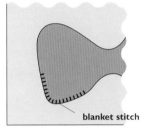

blanket stitch

> **tip**
>
> *Here's an alternative if you prefer a less time-consuming method for finishing the appliqués: Use size .004 monofilament nylon thread as the top thread in your sewing machine. This invisible thread saves time—you don't need to constantly change thread color to match the appliqués—and can hide imperfections in stitching. Be sure to adjust the machine tension so the bottom thread is not visible on top. You may need to loosen the top tension slightly.*

HAND APPLIQUÉ

If you prefer to hand stitch rather than fuse the appliqué shapes, reverse the appliqué patterns and make templates as described on page 44.

Place the template right side up on the right side of the appropriate appliqué fabric. Trace the template onto the fabric using a pencil or erasable fabric marker of your choice. Cut out the fabric shape, adding a ¼″-wide turn-under allowance.

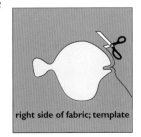

right side of fabric; template

Add a ¼" turn-under allowance to cut shapes.

Refer to the quilt photo and/or appliqué placement diagram in the project instructions to arrange the fabric pieces on the appliqué background. Fold under the fabric on the drawn line as you appliqué the shapes to the background, using a single strand of matching-colored thread and a blind or hem stitch.

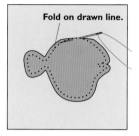

Fold on drawn line.

Match thread to color of appliqué shape.

EMBROIDERY STITCHES

Some quilts in this book feature simple, whimsical embroidered details. Refer to the following diagrams for assistance in creating the necessary stitches.

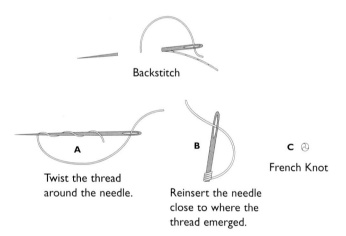

Backstitch

A
Twist the thread around the needle.

B
Reinsert the needle close to where the thread emerged.

C
French Knot

ADDING BORDERS

Many of the quilts in this book include borders with square-cut corners. These are the easiest of all borders to apply. The individual project instructions tell you how many strips to cut.

1. Measure the quilt top through the center from top to bottom. Cut 2 border strips to that length, piecing them if necessary. Pin the strips to the sides of the quilt top, with right sides together. Match the centers and ends of the strips to the center and ends of the quilt top, easing if necessary. Sew the border strips to the sides of the quilt top with ¼"-wide seams. Press as instructed, usually toward the border strips.

2. Measure the quilt through the center from side to side, including the borders you've just added. Repeat Step 1 to cut, pin, and sew the strips to the top and bottom of the quilt. Press.

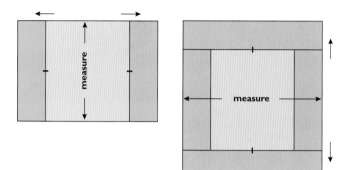

measure

measure

CHOOSING THE BATTING

There are many different types of batting including cotton, polyester, cotton-polyester blends, and wool—all in various "lofts" or thicknesses. Make your decision based on how and how much you intend to quilt, how the quilt will be used and cared for, and your own personal preferences. If you are unfamiliar with the various options and are not sure what type of batting will be best for your quilt, ask at your local quilt shop.

You can purchase batting either prepackaged or by the yard. Whichever you choose, you will want the batting at least 4" larger than your quilt top on all sides.

PREPARING THE QUILT BACKING

As with the batting, you'll want the backing fabric to be at least 4" larger than the quilt top on all sides. In most cases, you will need to seam the backing to have a large enough piece. Prewash the fabric and remove the selvages before dividing and piecing the backing fabric. To economize, you can piece the backing with vertical or horizontal seams, and include any fabrics or blocks in your collection.

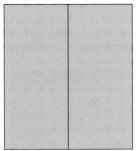
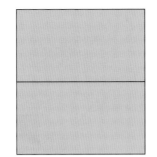

Backing with a vertical seam   Backing with a horizontal seam

BASTING THE QUILT

If you plan to machine quilt, pin-baste the quilt layers together with safety pins placed approximately 6″ apart. Begin in the center and pin toward the edges, first in vertical rows and then in horizontal rows to form a grid.

If you plan to hand quilt, baste the layers together using a long needle and a single, knotted strand of contrasting-colored thread. Begin in the center and stitch toward the edges, first in vertical rows and then in horizontal rows to form a grid. Lines of basting should be no more than 4″ apart. Finish by basting around the outside edges of the quilt.

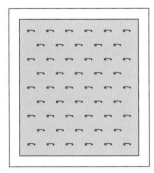
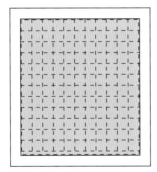

Pin basting for machine quilting   Thread basting for hand quilting

QUILTING

Quilting, whether done by machine (as for all the quilts in this book) or by hand, enhances the pieced and appliquéd designs. You may choose to quilt in-the-ditch; outline (or echo) the pieced and appliquéd motifs; trace designs from books, magazines, or stencils; or create your own designs. Use standard-weight quilting thread in colors that blend with your background fabrics. This way the quilting will enhance, rather than detract from the colorful combinations in the quilt designs.

Quilting in-the-ditch   Outline quilting

When you've finished the quilting, trim the backing and batting even with the quilt top.

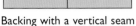

trim excess

BINDING

I cut my binding strips 3″ wide on the straight grain of the fabric. The instructions for each quilt tell you the number of strips you'll need to cut.

1. Sew the strips together to make one continuous binding strip. Press the seams open, and then press the entire strip in half lengthwise, with wrong sides together.

2. Align the raw edges of the binding with the raw edges of the quilt top. Starting a few inches from the beginning of the strip and near the middle of one of the sides of the quilt, stitch the binding to the quilt through all layers, with a ¼″-wide seam.

3. Stop sewing with a backstitch ¼" from the first corner. Lift the presser foot and needle. Rotate the quilt one-quarter turn. Fold the binding at a right angle so it extends straight above the quilt, and then fold down the binding even with the raw edge of the next side of the quilt top. Resume sewing at the folded edge, mitering each corner in this way as you come to it. Stop stitching approximately 4" from the starting end of the binding.

4. To finish the binding, unfold the starting end and turn under ¼" to create a finished edge; refold. Lay the end of the binding over the folded starting end. Finish stitching the ¼" seam and trim the excess binding strip, leaving an overlap of approximately ½".

5. Fold the binding strip over the raw edge of the quilt to the quilt back, covering the machine stitching. Hand stitch the binding to the quilt with matching-colored thread, mitering the corners.

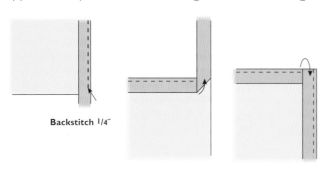

Backstitch 1/4"

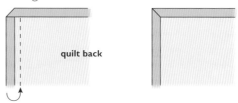

quilt back

ABOUT THE AUTHOR

Carol Burniston grew up with five sisters, a brother, and one Bernina sewing machine in a home that abounded with creativity. Her first quilt, made when she was nineteen while attending Utah State University, was a crazy quilt filled with lots of velvet and psychedelic polyester. A few years later, married with two small children and living in the Trinity Mountains in northern California, Carol opened a fabric store and began quilting in earnest.

Carol's sisters, Barbara Brandeburg and Teri Christopherson, have been successful book authors for a number of years. With their encouragement, Carol designed several projects for them. It didn't take long for Carol to find her own lighthearted, playful style. Another of Carol's sisters, Janet Murdock, has a longarm quilting business. She machine quilted all the projects for this, Carol's first book.